HOPE FOR LASTING CHANGE

Meeting Today's Problems with the Eternal Power of the Gospel

By Samuel Stephens

Copyright 2021 © Association of Certified Biblical Counselors

All rights reserved.

ISBN: 9781737810759

Association of Certified Biblical Counselors

As we face the issues of sin and suffering in a broken world, we all need wisdom from God. Thankfully, the Lord has given us all that we need for life and godliness through His sufficient Word (2 Peter 1:3; 2 Timothy 3:16).

ACBC's Truth in Love resources are designed to bring the rich truth of God's character and promises to bear on the problems people face in everyday life. As you walk with others, seeking to minister the very words of God to them, we pray this booklet will be a resource that points you back to His truth and equips you to admonish the idle, encourage the fainthearted, and help the weak (1 Thessalonians 5:14).

Author
Samuel Stephens is Director of Training Center Certification at the Association of Certified Biblical Counselors and Assistant Professor of Biblical Counseling at Midwestern Baptist Theological Seminary.

There is one reason why people seek counseling and it is *not* because things are going well. While the problems our counselees bring to us are often multifaceted and differ from person to person, the consistent theme that we must be prepared for as biblical counselors is the *need* our counselees have to change. Paul recognized this *universal need* when he spoke about how Jesus Christ died for us "so that they who live might no longer live for themselves, but for Him who died and rose again on their behalf" (2 Corinthians 5:15).

As counselors, we recognize this need to change because we have the same need. In our unregenerate state, our hearts are not oriented around God. Our mind, will, and desires bear the mark of the curse (Jeremiah 17:9). We are self-deceived, arrogant, and vain. We are unable to accept, and often openly reject, the ways of God (1 Corinthians 2:14). We are without hope and without God (Ephesians 2:12).

No matter how you cut it, that is a pretty bleak scenario. But this is not where the story ends.

We who were once far away and lost in our sins have been brought near through Jesus Christ's substitutionary atonement on the cross

(Ephesians 2:13). The dead, deceitful, and unregenerate heart is replaced with one that beats for the King. We are new creatures with a new hope (2 Corinthians 5:17). We have qualitatively and substantially changed.[1]

Before moving forward, it is vital to remember that biblical counseling is directed to people who have these *new* hearts. Jay Adams provides a helpful perspective on this in *Sanctification and Counseling*:

> The object true Christian counselors have in view is to help counselees to honor and please God by bringing about the changes in counselees that He requires. Christian counseling cannot be provided for the unregenerate since it is impossible for them to honor or please God. So wise counselors make this clear and evangelize rather than counsel unbelievers. Such counselors will not settle for outward change that does not flow and correspond to an inward change of heart.[2]

---

[1] This is not to speak of something repurposed or refurbished. This is not a mere whitewashing of an old heart. The newness spoken of in this verse is unprecedented, uncommon, and supernatural. In effect, God has replaced our stone-cold and dead hearts with ones that are dynamic and alive (Ezekiel 36:26).

[2] Jay Adams, *Sanctification and Counseling* (Cordova, TN:

While Jesus Christ provides the ultimate cure-all to heal the sin-sick heart, we as counselors (and as human beings) know that the need for change does not go away even after we are born again. Allow me to ask you a personal question. Since your conversion, have you ever felt stuck and in need of change in a particular area of your life? You may know the feeling quite well. After tirelessly attempting to move forward, you just end up spinning your wheels and sinking deeper in a pit (often with mud on your face). Situations like this leave us feeling frustrated and hopeless. What makes matters worse is that many of the pits in which we find ourselves are of our own making. Likewise, our counselees come to us because many of them perceive at some level that something needs to change.

Some are burdened by anxiety, worry, or fear of the world around them. They search for ways to find anything resembling peace so they can escape the ill-effects of constant worry. A peace-of-mind is not the only thing absent in a worrier. There are negative relational, spiritual, and physical consequences that worry can have on a person.

INS Publishing, 2020), 92. I am greatly indebted to Adams in considering the powerful resource that God has granted to the counselor in the form of a counselee's regenerate heart.

Others may be stirred to anger at the drop of a hat. These people are quick to "put walls up" when they feel threatened or challenged. They often take offense when no offense is intended. Many techniques are available in which unhappy and angry people can try to "channel" their anger in "healthy" ways. But, in the end, these solutions do not lead to real or lasting change and often they find that a root of bitterness remains.

Still others find themselves unmotivated and lacking any direction for their lives. Somewhere along the way, life has become all about the "rat race" and genuine meaning and purpose in life seems elusive. Work drags on and family life is seen as tedious and inconvenient.

Can you identify an area in your counselee's life that needs change? If so, how should we as biblical counselors go about showing them the true *need* for change as well as the *means* of that change? As we consider this vital task, it is important to consider that there are essentially two approaches to change. In the short term, both options *seem* to offer resolutions to life's difficulties, but only one can offer true and lasting hope. A man-centered and psychotherapeutic approach only offers a temporary and surface-level quick fix and should be avoided by biblical counselors.

Unfortunately, many Christians seek to utilize and integrate such methods in their counseling. We must strive to avoid such surface-level and faulty attempts and instead seek a route that is theological and biblical. Only an approach derived from Scripture can capitalize on the new hearts of our counselees and rely upon the power of the Holy Spirit and the church.

The Quick Fix – A Therapeutic Approach to Change

If you have been in a bookstore recently, you have most likely seen the self-help section. Books included in this ever-expanding genre promise easy steps and quick results for change in areas including finance, relationships, diet/health, career development, and personality flaws. While the topics and issues brought up in these texts are varied, there are three common themes found in what I call the *Quick Fix* approach.[3]

---

[3] Biblical counselors need to be aware that even though much of this approach is secular in nature, there are many within Christian and biblical counseling circles who attempt to either partially or fully utilize some aspects of this method.

The Quick Fix is Me-Centered

The world attempts many solutions in meeting the desire for change that people have. However, most of these focus and rely upon the personal abilities, resources, and drive of the very person seeking change. How can someone whose life is marked by selfishness, confusion, anger, and vain conceit find a solution leading to lasting change in their own power? The answer is, they can't.

Scripture speaks to the natural "me-ism" that is inherent in every person.[4] The Old Testament depicted the motivations of the chosen people of Israel who desired the ways of the world over the ways of God. Their man-centered attitude could be summed up in that "everyone did what was right in his own eyes" (Judges 21:25). King Solomon echoed this sentiment when he wrote, "The way of the fool is right in his own eyes, but a wise man is he who listens to counsel" (Proverbs 12:15). Speaking of a self-consumed life outside of Jesus Christ, the Apostle Paul said, "Among them we too all formerly lived in the lusts of our flesh, indulging the desires of the flesh and of the mind, and were by nature children of wrath" (Ephesians 2:3).

---

[4] This is the default status of the unregenerate, but even as a regenerate person, the struggle with the old man is ongoing.

The Bible makes it clear that man's sinful inclination is the "me-centered" life. Ironically, while so much advice from this approach leans towards self-help, the "self" turns out to be the actual culprit behind our very need of change.

The Quick Fix is Temporary

The second characteristic of this approach to change is that it only offers short-term relief. A couple once came to me seeking marriage counseling. Both the husband and wife brought a laundry list of concerns and complaints about the other. The wife pointed out, "He is uncaring and speaks harshly to me!" Her husband would quickly respond, "She never cooks dinner or cares about how the house looks!" The accusations kept flying. What they wanted from me was to provide a list of steps for them to take to address these problems. I could say to the husband, "Speak gently and lovingly to your wife. Think before you speak to show her that you love her." To the wife, I might say, "Make an attempt to keep the house tidy. The way you keep house will show your husband that you care for him."

On face value, this counsel is not too far off the mark. If it is followed by both spouses, one would imagine that a certain level of stress or strain between the couple would be lessened. They may even begin "feeling better" about the state of their marriage. However, only counseling toward obvious issues does not take into account the more serious and foundational problems that often lie beneath the surface.

When only surface-level problems are addressed, the best one can hope for is change for a season. In the Scriptures, Jesus spoke of two different men. One man was concerned with addressing the visible, surface-level issues, while the other man understood that no matter how good everything looked on the outside, if the foundation was not solid, his life would all come crashing down. In Matthew 7:24-27, Jesus said:

> Therefore everyone who hears these words of Mine and acts on them, may be compared to a wise man who built his house on the rock. And the rain fell, and the floods came, and the winds blew and slammed against that house; and yet it did not fall, for it had been founded on the rock. Everyone who hears these words of Mine and does not act on them, will be like a foolish man who built his house on the sand. The rain fell, and the floods

came, and the winds blew and slammed against that house; and it fell—and great was its fall.

This teaching parallels with a proverb of Solomon that states, "When the whirlwind passes, the wicked is no more, but the righteous has an everlasting foundation" (Proverbs 10:25). The point here is that when we attempt to address our need for change using the latest self-help techniques or therapeutic approaches, we are only addressing the fruit problems and not the root problems. This will only lead to temporary change and false hope.

The Quick Fix is Habit Focused[5]

Habits are God-given and good. Think about it. When was the last time that you had to consciously think about checking your mirrors or applying the break when you see a yellow or red light? When was the last time you had to think about walking or brushing your teeth? Habits help us accomplish everyday tasks efficiently and without major concern. Habits are also a

---

[5] What I am referring to here is surface-level, mechanical, and technique-driven habits. I distinguish and contrast this approach from a biblical approach to habituation, which seeks to instill God-honoring practices in the lives of our counselees.

blessing to us as we make it a faithful practice to engage in various spiritual disciplines and seek to die to ourselves daily. The more often that we make this a priority and press into the power of the Spirit of God, we live the holy lives that Christ died for us to live. Habits are good.[6]

On the other hand, habits can also be bad. People who are dominated by anger and bitterness do not become this way overnight. This type of attitude, and its related behavior, has been embraced to the point that reacting in anger has become second nature. Those who feel directionless and purposeless have allowed themselves to become enamored by temporary things, from spending countless hours on social media to overcommitting every resource toward career advancement. Self-seeking motivations create self-serving habits. John warns us that our actions may betray us, "By this the children of God and the children of the devil are obvious: anyone who does not practice righteousness is not of God, nor the one who does not love his brother" (1 John 3:10). Just because habits have been replaced does not necessarily mean that the heart has been ad-

---

[6] The doctrine of repentance has daily implications for us. As Christians, we are constantly in need of confession and repentance, which should lead us to living holier lives. These types of efforts can be called habitual, but it can never be disconnected from the heart.

dressed. It is a psychotherapeutic approach, not a biblical one, that promotes coping mechanisms and behavioristic techniques as solutions to problems without recognizing that these problems originate from the heart (Proverbs 4:23).

The Eternal Remedy – The Biblical Blessing of Sanctification

Is the Bible sufficient in identifying our counselee's problems and providing a remedy to their problems? When confronted with these questions, many may not be sure how to answer. After all, the Bible is a religious book and is only concerned with "religious matters," right? The truth is that the Bible was given to us by God in order that we may live in such a way that pleases Him and brings Him glory. It speaks to the need for change and is replete with examples of everyday people who needed change but could not accomplish it on their own. When our counselees come to us with their desire to change, they will need guidance in not only knowing *what* change should look like, but also *how* this change can take place and *why* it is necessary.

Concerning the power of Scripture and its impact on the lives of everyday people, Paul stated, "All Scripture is inspired by God and profitable for teaching, for reproof, for correction, for training in righteousness; so that the man of God may be adequate, equipped for every good work" (2 Timothy 3:16-17). There are countless passages through the Old and New Testaments that testify to the Bible's reliability, purpose, and power in effecting life-altering change. The Word of God is perfect and is able to restore man's soul (Psalm 19:7), it is a light that illuminates our darkness (Psalm 119:105; Proverbs 6:21-23), it is effective in accomplishing God's will (Isaiah 55:11); it is well established and is not swayed by popular opinion (John 1:1), and among other things, it provides hope (Romans 15:4).

The multitude of psychotherapeutic remedies attempts to cure what ails our counselees. A *remedy*, by definition, denotes healing, restorative cure, and relief from disease or disorder. However, no matter how effective a medical intervention is in treating bodily illness or how psychological counseling seems to promote emotional well-being, these both eventually succumb to the reality of mortality. In stark contrast to symptomatic relief, the Scriptures speak to an *Eternal Remedy* for the sin that plagues all people (Genesis 3:14-19; Jeremiah 17:9-10; Romans 3:23; 6:23-24).

The Eternal Remedy is Christ-Centered

As opposed to the *Quick Fix* approach to change, the *Eternal Remedy* is centered on the person and work of Jesus Christ. Paul described the natural posture of man's heart and motivation before salvation. He said, "For we also once were foolish ourselves, disobedient, deceived, enslaved to various lusts and pleasures, spending our life in malice and envy, hateful, hating one another" (Titus 3:3).

Our extreme "me-ism" is the major contributing factor to most of the problems, roadblocks, and messes we find ourselves in. The angry person, while attempting to convince himself that he does not want to be angry, actually does wish to remain angry. Anger and bitterness lure us into false security and power. Anxious people do not want to really give up their anxious thoughts because it is an attempt at being God. If they can comprehend, manipulate, or reason through any situation, it gives them a false sense of understanding and control. All men and women are naturally self-centered and self-focused and thus they have "no hope" and are "without God in this world" (Ephesians 2:12).

Instead of being conformed to the image of Jesus Christ, those who are self-centered are being formed in the image of themselves. The *Quick Fix* solutions are not solutions at all. This approach is merely man's attempt at "fixing" his sin problem. However, Scripture tells us that only Christ could pay the sin-debt that we owe to God. After sharing the hopeless message of the depths of man's sin, Paul finishes his statement in Titus 3:4-5 on an encouraging note:

> But when the kindness of God our Savior and His love for mankind appeared, He saved us, not on the basis of deeds which we have done in righteousness, but according to His mercy, by the washing of regeneration and renewing by the Holy Spirit.

The forgiveness of God through faith in Christ is available to all men and is the first step of encountering the remedy of the sin-sick soul.

The Eternal Remedy is Permanent

Paul mentions in Titus 3:5-7 that when we confess Jesus as our Lord and Savior, we receive His Holy Spirit. This passage says that the Holy Spirit *renews* us. The presence of the Spirit of God in the lives of men and women is a powerful testimony of God's faithfulness and commitment in the work of making us holy (Philippians 1:6). His regeneration and renewal of our hearts is the most permanent type of change available to us. It is not like the surface-level and temporary change that a man-centered approach offers. Instead, it refers to a complete renovation of the mind, will, and desires of our hearts.

The heart renovation that Christ begins, He promises He will continue. The presence of the Holy Spirit within the life a born-again disciple of Jesus is a seal of permanence and inheritance (Ephesians 1:13-14). Paul's confidence was not in his credentials but in the fact that Christ "sealed us and gave us the Spirit in our hearts as a pledge" (2 Corinthians 1:22). The spiritual transaction that takes place at salvation cannot be undone. Believers are "new creatures" with the old life, the one of self-centered motivations, passing away (2 Corinthians 5:17; Galatians 2:20). Similarly, the spiritual renovation that begins at salvation is guaranteed to continue in our daily lives.

What does this mean for our counselees (and for us)?

It means that we are no longer obligated to remain angry and bitter. Instead, through the power of the Holy Spirit, our counselees can choose to not take up offenses, to forgive, and to love the unlovable. It means that they are not under obligation to alcohol or drug abuse. Instead, with the support of the church, they can withstand temptations and flee from unholy things. It means that they are not bound to view pornography, succumb to same-sex desires, or commit adultery. Instead, through the inspiration of the Scriptures, the loving care of the church, and the power of the Holy Spirit, they can please God in their thoughts, words, and deeds. In short, they can experience *life-changing* change (Romans 8:1).

The Eternal Remedy is Heart-Focused

The final point in considering the *Eternal Remedy* is the prominence the heart plays in the process of change. Man-centered promises for change never address the heart because these approaches discount its importance. As described in Scripture, the heart is the seat of man's spiritual life which, in turn, holds sway over all other aspects of his life including his emotions, thoughts, and actions.[7]

---

[7] For a thorough grasp on what part the heart plays in our sanctification see the following: A. Craig Troxel, *With All Your Heart: Orienting your Mind, Desires, and Will*

Moses noted the importance of the heart as he recorded the early history of mankind in Genesis. "Then the Lord saw that the wickedness of man was great on the earth, and that every intent of the thoughts of his heart was only evil continually" (Genesis 6:5). The link between the posture of the heart and the quality of man's actions is prevalent throughout Scripture. Speaking in Luke 6:43-45, Jesus referred to the importance of the heart as He spoke to His disciples:

> For there is no good tree which produced bad fruit, nor, on the other hand, a bad tree which produced good fruit. For each tree is known by its own fruit. For men do not gather figs from thorns, nor do they pick grapes from a briar bush. The good man out of the good treasure of his heart brings fort what is good; and the evil man out of the evil treasure brings forth what is evil; for his mouth speaks from that which fills his heart.

The "good treasure" that is mentioned by Jesus in this passage is not of man's own making. It is a treasure placed there by God Himself. Paul described this in 2 Corinthians 4:7, "But we

---

Toward Christ (Wheaton, Ill: Crossway, 2020) and Brian Borgman, *Faith and Feelings: Cultivating Godly Emotions in the Christian Life* (Wheaton, Ill; Crossway, 2009).

have this treasure in earthen vessels, so that the surpassing greatness of the power will be of God and not from ourselves." In this passage, Paul empathizes with the Christians at Corinth in that he too experienced great persecution, strife, and conflict on behalf of Christ and the Gospel. Nevertheless, he did not allow such turmoil to determine his actions; instead, he did not lose heart, but was reminded that while his struggles were temporary, his soul was eternal (2 Corinthians 4:16). As you consider your counselee's deep-seated need for change, consider the "things which are not seen" first, for these things hold an eternal weight (2 Corinthians 4:18).

For change to be genuine, you must consider the state of your counselee's heart. James 1:23-25 points to the importance behind identifying the motivation the heart:

> For if anyone is a hearer of the word and not a doer, he is like a man who looks at his natural face in a mirror; for once he has looked at himself and gone away, he has immediately forgotten what kind of person he was. But one who looks intently at the perfect law of liberty, and abides by it, not having become a forgetful

> hearer but an effectual doer, this man will be blessed in what he does.

Hearers are aware that there is a problem but are unwilling to do the hard work of self-confrontation which leads to change. Instead they desire to remain the judges and arbiters of their own life choices and circumstances. Doers confess their inability to enact lasting change. They turn to Scripture, what James calls the perfect law of liberty, which accurately reveals the inner ugliness of our self-centeredness. It does not shield our counselees from the fact that they cannot change or save themselves and that spiritual heart surgery is necessary. It also provides the corrective necessary for change to take place. If you conclude that your counselee's behaviors, habits, words, or actions are in need of change, be assured that their heart is indeed in need of renovation.

A Final Word

Before the creation of the world, God, in His goodness and sovereignty, knew that we would find ourselves in need of change. Therefore, He provided the Bible to us as both an accurate mirror of our soul and as a surgical instrument to aid us in the change process.

What change needs to take place?

Jesus provided the standard for which all of life should be oriented and established. Quoting the Old Testament, Jesus said, "'YOU SHALL LOVE THE LORD YOUR GOD WITH ALL YOUR HEART, AND WITH ALL YOUR SOUL, AND WITH ALL YOUR MIND.' This is the great and foremost commandment. The second is like it, 'YOU SHALL LOVE YOUR NEIGHBOR AS YOURSELF.' On these two commandments depend the whole Law and the Prophets" (Matthew 22:37-39). If your counselee is unable to follow this command perfectly, then they are in need of change.

While every person's situation calls for particular changes, the ultimate goal of change for all people is provided in that we were created to love God and love our neighbor. Nowhere in Scripture is there a command to love ourselves.[8] However, many of our counselees spend their days seeking after the pleasures of this world with no thought of the God who created us to love and worship Him (1 John 2:15-17). The call of the Gospel is a call to deny self, take up the cross of Jesus, and follow after Him (Mark 8:34). Jesus asked this to His disciples, "For what does it profit a man to gain the whole world, and for-

---

[8] It is in this area that the psychotherapeutic influences upon so-called Christian counseling can be the most clearly seen.

feit his soul?" (Mark 8:36). Only by placing their trust in Jesus to refine them from the inside out, can our counselees truly experience life-altering change (Romans 10:9-13).

How does change take place?

Once our spiritual need has been identified through the trustworthy lens of Scripture, the process of change can take place. As discussed in this resource, there are two very different approaches to change. The first is me-centered, temporary, and focuses on behavioral modification, while the other is Christ-centered, permanent, and focuses on the condition of the heart.

Jesus Christ is our eternal remedy and the Bible is the precision instrument that cuts away everything that dishonors God and others. Hebrews 4:12 states, "For the word of God is living and active and sharper than any two-edged sword, and piercing as far as the division of soul and spirit, of both joints and marrow, and able to judge the thoughts and intentions of the heart." Deep-rooted change is possible and available to those willing to allow God, in His Son, through the Spirit, to purify their hearts as silver is refined through fire (Psalm 66:10; Isaiah 48:10; 1

Peter 1:7). Then you will become a "vessel for honor, sanctified, useful to the Master, prepared for every good work (2 Timothy 2:21).

PART OF THE BIBLICAL SOLUTIONS SERIES

More Coming Soon

GET MORE AT:
biblicalcounseling.com/biblicalsolutions

Biblical Solutions for the Problems People Face

The Association of Certified Biblical Counselors is committed to championing the sufficiency of Scripture for the Church as she engages the problems people face, speaking the truth in love. Christians have the responsibility to bring the truth of God to bear on the problems of everyday life, and to embody that truth in a life of love.

At ACBC, we seek to strengthen the Church to speak the truth in love by providing a quality training and certification process, a global network of like-minded individuals and institutions, and a source of practical and biblical resources for the Church.

In short, we seek to bring *biblical solutions for the problems people face*, upholding that the method God has given to do this is *truth in love*.

Find all our ACBC resources at www.biblicalcounseling.com.